WALKING DOWN
THE SENSORY STRIP

sejal akerkar

ISBN: 9780578812199

Cover Illustration by: Sejal Akerkar

this book is dedicated to my parents, who have pushed me to become a better person in this modifying world. thank you for being my inspiration to publish this collection. i love you.

beneficiary

all of the proceeds from this book will be donated to Udayan Care, a
non-profit organization. they strive to improve the lives of orphaned
and abandoned children and provide education and mentoring to
poor girls in india. my family has been associated with Udayan Care
for nine years. we have visited and celebrated with them. the
connections i have with some of the girls and their stories at Udayan
Care have inspired me to donate the proceeds of this collection to
them and their fellow sisters and brothers. these donations will help
educate the children of Udayan Care and allow them to express
themselves in society like i am.

contents

my dictionary 3

downward tunnel 23

monarch archway 75

piercing berry 99

quiet forest 121

crystal splash 163

welcome to my sensory strip. a path that we can walk down together. come back or stop when you need, it's a bumpy ride. enjoy.

my dictionary

use these to pinpoint feelings you could never define

anemoia

(n) de ja vu of memories you cannot recall in your living present but could possibly be sent from the past

heartworm

(n) a feeling that two people are still grasping for each other's air

needed their lungs to circulate and still do

unfinished air

they thought they had already swallowed

kairosclerosis

(n) the moment you realize that you are living

the dream you have replayed in your head

every night before you go to sleep

savoring the sugary taste of cotton candy

when you know the fluff will disintegrate through your taste buds

and you will be back to dreaming again

kenopsia

(n) the dead but almost waking

unreal atmosphere of a place

previous life feels

now forlorn and forgotten

catoptric tristesse

(n) the distraught feeling that you will never receive the book of

thoughts that enlace the insides of people's minds when they think of
you

whether heart rushing

blood boiling

you will never know

if you even cross their mind at all

mimeomia

(n) the intimidation of a specific stereotype that you fit into
even if you do not want to
you will always fit that stereotype

monachopsis

(n) a feeling of displacement in an undesired quadrant of the world

nighthawk

(n) a recurring thought that only seems to strike you late at night

an overdue task

a nagging guilt

a looming

and shapeless future

always coming back within those sheets

stars reflecting the twinkle into your cerebrum

pâro

(n) the feeling that even though you trudge strenuously
through sandy desperation
the camel only moved a foot when miles
of dunes role through your lens

downward tunnel

the beginning of our path

6:34 am

my body rolls out of bed

but i'm still tucked under the sheets

actions + words = love

come see me

because you say you miss me

word on the street says you have all the time in the world

the sidewalks talk to me

you walked here

i read the calligraphic precipitation

the misty sky writes it out in clouds

either take the effort

or don't say it at all

before you say something that

you can't pull through with

at night

is everything at night
just better
and more enjoyable
when you're sleep deprived

the talks about
loves and life

the spontaneous decisions that
could or could not
change your life
forever

the laughs
about stupid things

the crying
also
probably about stupid things

the darkness can
give you a different
sense of warmth

empty out the bottle

the first time i saw a boy cry was on the playground

after he skinned his knee playing tag on those deadly wood chips

boys cry i grew up

realized boys don't like to cry

why?

they feel the need to be strong

not sensitive the next time

i saw a boy cry was after he got in trouble

imagining what his parents would think of him

boys cry boys show emotion

how does it feel suppressing all your tears into one tiny bottle at the pit of your stomach

the last time i saw a boy cry was after losing someone he loved

to a silly mistake

boys cry

boys are vulnerable

they are strong

it is okay

for the bottle to spill once in a while

gone

why keep searching
when you know it isn't there
you are looking for a sign
someone to tell you to go back
when you know you should go on

it's gone
your go-to, gone
your best friend, gone
your person, gone

you want those memories back
to remind you of the carefree times
you want it back
the person you
once knew
is gone

they are the same on the outside

same eyes

same hair

same lips

same voice

but different insides

they are different

stopped loving you

stopped showing interest

stopped trying

we were not the same

you thought

am i the wrong

in all the right that they were

you needed to change

for them to love you

but it was always them

they weren't the same person

anymore

you thought you knew them

right?

but things can change

and something was off

you both knew it

it ended

it had to

it was going to

but you both weren't ready to give up something you

once loved

and we drown ourselves

in tears waiting

for the old them

to come back

the new them moved on

and you didn't

you could not

do it anymore

we make excuses for the people we love

just to keep them in our lives

for a bit longer

i come home

sit on the bed

and think about

the greatness that lied with in

the kind soul

the rare heart

the thoughtful mind

the beautiful face

but even more beautiful

personality

so many memories i want

to relive with that soul

but it

disappeared

slowly

and if the soul is in

the wrong person

it leaves

i caught your good soul for

a millisecond

before it left

i felt like i had won the

lottery of souls

until it vanished from

the person

i loved

and then it was the

body left

which was fine

until i realized that i should

be chasing the soul

not the person

and never settle for just average

every mistake took

a bite out of their soul

they could never love me

the way i wanted them to

that is when i knew

i had to let go

interior of a tea light

injected at last life

when liquid wax is fresh

hot essence boils in my veins as

i doggie paddle around a shrinking metal

swimming pool

trying not to be engulfed into

the fast hardening substance

the wick guiding me out as

i retrieve my breath

and stare back at the

frozen pond of a tea light

labels

you can physically filter out that person

that fit the label

for others to shuffle through

but you can never replace that person

the one that made you realize

they were the only one for you

you can never internally filter that person out

of your heart

your gut

she knew from the start
they were going to hurt me
and i was going to fall for it
trust her
she is always right

letting go

that one moment
the choices we made
ruined everything

i loved us so much
how could we mess it up
i said

how did it go wrong
fast
just like that

how did we let it fall
go down hill
that we gave up

series of events
that just made our
friendship crumble

losing you was not
as painful
as choosing
to let go

miracle fruit

i cannot reach you

i can't make you spill all your

secrets onto the chopping board

even though

i'm the only one who has the knife

and everyone is jealous

but i am still searching

gutting you inside and out

trying to taste your magic

like a rare seed

that only i have

i understand you don't want to share the pit inside

because i have never shared mine with you

mistimed love

you lose the people that start to love you
after you stopped loving them

toxic guide

you cannot make someone like you

become their person

let them want you

distance yourself

they become vulnerable

and they will know no other person like you

flashback memories

either break you

or bring you joy

it is exciting

looking back

laughing at what you lacked

reading all the paragraphs

you sent at 3 am

the fast food runs

after long days

showing the midnight daze

of what life used to be like

powerful empire

i convince myself that i do not need you anymore

you broke me

and i pieced myself back together

all me

i created my own

powerful empire

i have fought wars

all without you

i have done it all by myself

but i still imagine

what if you had stayed

we built up our own

powerful empire

and we took over the whole world

we won every war

the fighting powered by our friendship

you would have been my battleship

we could have overcome

teenage humor

funny how we become sad

when remembering happy things

tunnel scene

i stand on the moving train

electricity in my veins

head wrapped around my body

body wrapped around my brain

the ibis approaches

i am ready i say

to see the other side

the tunnel doorway

what are you doing

i have lost my faith in the new

that is why i go back to the ones i trusted

because i'm scared

that if i meet new ones

they are going to do the

exact same thing you did to me

whoever you want this to be

the voice of the devil

gives fake hugs

lectures failure

and fights with your pain

drives you to succeed

teaches you to be a princess

and always strangles your freedom

winning arguments

do not ever raise your voice with me

because i will beat you down

tear your thoughts

manipulate your mind

rip up your arguments

and eliminate your words

under the cold trickling water

coming from my shower head

how i know i'm falling

i reach the cliff

people behind me

they watch me trip

spinning on my toes

grasping for a hand

and everyone just

watches as i

see their faces disappear

i realize

i'm falling

swan diving down the deep

hole of left-over pins and needles

with no sight of return

monarch archway

caterpillar's personal advice to you

a characteristic recipe

20% integrity towards goals

15% loyalty towards others

15% devotion towards culture

40% loving towards yourself

10% self-control towards relationships

these are my ingredients to life

master your recipe

advice to a butterfly

do not change the color of your wings

only change because you want to

you don't need to fit society's standards

you just need to fit your own

comparing to a monarch won't make you one

live in that skin of a polished caterpillar

you cocooned so they could

see you fly

comparing

i compare my situations to everyone

some people grow faster than i do

and i need to accept that

people move on faster than others

i need to take the time i need

people receive things they don't deserve

i can work hard for the things i want

nobody is the same

different opportunities come with different chances

that is the scale of life

only thing you have done for me

i have these

sticky notes

bright orange sticky notes

that i keep beside

my bed

to write down things that i

need to do in the morning

but after

the reminders have turned into poems

thank you

for being my inspiration

patience

please

keep waiting

good times will come

just like you remember them

may the world never hurt you again

writing a collection

poetry should never be rushed

take your time

before you waste it

writing nonsense

that you don't love

poetry

when i started writing poems

it was to take my thoughts

and paint them on a canvas

full of delectable words

but it is also bringing me

back to you

it looks like it is helping

father figure

it will be nostalgic looking into the eyes of my partner

because i will have already seen them every day since i was born

in the pupils of my father

ready, set, go

why do we practice
self-care

are we getting
ready for a game

or a tournament

why don't we just
do self-care

no need to practice
taking care of
oneself

trust the process

practice makes better

better equals progress

mini tsnami

your wave of happiness

will come

you need to have happiness

before it can reach the shore of others

piercing berry

self-image is the thorn you must swallow to taste the sweetness

a picture can deceive the eye

models are being shown with added reshaping

real people

not show dolls

ignore the pictures because they are modified

masks are not painted on the inside

paint can only portray so much beauty

you never know what could be going on

behind the veil of a pretty face

home

walking the streets of haryana

is a giant

jewels melt out of her hair

she wants restoration

back to her people

who eat up the emerald and ruby

like live flesh

dripping blood of soldiers

serving our country

as the gates are left open

ajar

we are ready they say

for peace

they finally understand

Gandhi was an equal

parading down for the last time

delhi is where i grew up

it is ghar

popsicle

women are like popsicles to you

they have frozen all this flavor

for you to just suck it up

to maneuver your tongue

lick the droplets of juice that sit on your hand and your shirt

they are all over you

and you make it messy

what is left

is a stick

and a joke written on her side

second generation immigrant

the Shiva on the counter

the tabla drums on Gandhi's wheel

the Ganesha on the stairwell

the photographs of delhi above the fireplace

everything i love comes from that place

but i don't want to be associated with them

it is beautiful

my grandparents came here to give me a better life

to acculturate

but all i want is to not be from that place

why do i stray away from my culture

leave a part of myself behind

am i ashamed

trying to be more "american"

when diversity is what makes america

sejal sumangala akerkar

her name is

sejal sumangala akerkar

her name means

pure

she does not know her own full potential to be great

she thinks her hair is too thick

her name too foreign

and her skin too dark

she never saw what other

people cherished

no one ever told her being

different was okay

she forgets where she comes from

why her hair grows so fast

why she had an accent

if she could see her beauty

all along she would have known

that she didn't have to change

she would know her worth

she is more than just what

she thinks are her flaws

the gold woman

delicately decorating her lengthy figure

with gold

ringed hoops lay in her earlobes

made of gold

chain strung with diamonds

positions itself on top of her mighty podium

laced with gold

only gold makes her whole

which birthed her horrendous soul

the race

it is okay to be both

i know you don't want to

but you cannot make it disappear

you know that your skin color is darker

your hair a little thicker

your name a little longer

combine your two worlds

because you never know when

you might need one more than the other

thick hair

she tells me that there is hair in my armpits

she hands me a razor

she says that my upper lip hair is growing

she passes me wax strips

she exclaims that my eyebrows are touching

she takes me to get them threaded

she is a goddess of India

where thick jet-black hair grows everywhere

yet

she is telling me to get rid of it

like getting rid of who i am

the people of India

the basket of biscuits

that our mother kept in the car

is what her heart has to offer

biscuits fed to the little kids

selling toys

DVD's

barely tall enough to reach the window

the dirt implanted with their footsteps

and eyes as hopeful as she was

my mother fought

for them

she was

so many people's

mother

uni (brow)

things can come in ones and twos

just like your eyebrows

quiet forest

unnamed

unnamed #1

some people say

when you think about someone you miss

they are thinking about you too

but i think about you everyday

and i know you haven't thought of me once

unnamed #2

we want to stay sad

because we feel like it will

bring back the happiness

of the past

unnamed #3

am i quitting because i don't love it anymore
or because i don't want to try to be better

unnamed #4

you can hear when they say i love you

but you can feel all the times that they don't mean it

you have been hugged by someone

but you've never been embraced

unnamed #5

they are not as sweet

as they say they are

they will never be

able to feed you

what you need

because the roots

always affect

the fruit

unnamed #6

stop putting in effort

they will never be the person

you want them to be

you need to love them for who they are

or just not love them at all

unnamed #7

always treat them with respect

always end on good terms

you will

have peace of mind

unnamed #8

fall in love with you

you only need yourself

unnamed #9

i still want to know everything about you

even when

"i don't care"

unnamed #10

oh

you thought that you could just hurt me and run away

no

i'm going to hurt you too

because lying

is a two-person game my friend

unnamed #11

in the world where we sit on both of our beds

and talk for hours

is where you love me

tell me you love me

in our second world we have different friends

different lives

and not talk at all

we learn about things

we won't even remember tomorrow

but i want to learn about you

and i know i will remember that for a lifetime

don't quarantine me away from who you are in real life

because i only know you through our screens

unnamed #12

losing a best friend

is like losing a part of yourself

they helped you blossom

and without them you can't keep growing

they are the water to your roots

raining on you

pouring their heart and soul

into making you happy

they seep through you

unnoticed of the good change

but flagrant of what sets you apart

there are droughts

and as we swallow one last drop

we lose the sun

fueling the sunlight

unnamed #13

being blessed does not give you the blessing of happiness

you can have everything

and still feel like you have nothing

unnamed #14

you don't need to compare shapes

we are all wishing we were on the other side

too skinny

too fat

accept whom you are

and know that you are perfect

we are all on the same side

unnamed #15

you need to decide

i cannot just be your first choice

then suddenly your second

you cannot have me

then suddenly abandon me when you feel like it

choose to hold on

and when to let go

unnamed #16

every day is a first
firsts are celebrated
or looked down upon
firsts can be scary
or they can be exciting

a first is categorized in the book of life
they are the most
important
and the most memorable

memories known
to a single human being
most firsts are celebrated
at the beginning of life

your first step
your first word

you get older and accomplish

your first day of school

your first fight with a loved one

then things decrease

less firsts

you have done a lot

and now your firsts

are different

entering the fun years of being a teenager

your first party

your first kiss

these firsts are hard

but they get harder

your first acceptance letter

your first heartbreak

someone is always celebrating with you

your first drink

your first disappointment

entering adulthood

your first job

your first apartment

but amid the confusion and taxes

your first love

your first ring

and we come back to excitement

you feel young again

you are celebrated

your first house

your first child

more celebration

being thrown at you

from every direction possible

for the first time

instead of being celebrated

you become the person

that has helped celebrate

your firsts

the people that were
always there
to celebrate you
and your firsts

you are your child's
first celebrator
you are a parent

unnamed #17

someone poured honey

on my keyboard

the system holds the jar

begging for my delicacies

to type into my future

prying for an introduction

a body

a conclusion

my fingers are attached

forced words out of the tips

nail beds still sweet and sticky

crystal splash

in its natural nature

a stab you never intended

the evening bird looks in the window

expecting to look at something new

but he still looks at the same black widow

weaves her web she gazes at the sunrise view

every day she goes down her white web

he watches her delicately is he

reversing his rushed heart began to ebb

she watches every day from her fruit tree

she wrote songs to him with feathery silk

he only caught her stare not the message

he just licked her up like sweet buttermilk

but she tried warning him with a presage

she couldn't stop herself that watchful night

he died of first love from that dreadful bite

clouds

sometimes

clouds are sad

and gloomy

they sag down and make the world

distressed

they move with the earth

the sun shines through them

and creates a vortex

that pulls me into the mesmerizing

light of the sky

constructing wanderlust

that sparkles in my iris

in pursuit for more

of the frosty steam that

patrols the sky

mother earth

we are unappreciative of soil

instead of roses, tulips and lilies

we send her pollution, climate change and droughts

we harm her children

to produce meat and milk that pack our aisles

and she keeps quiet

does not say a word

never complains about what we have done

but she shakes her head in grief through earthquakes

she boils up inside through volcanos

she bursts with profuseness through tsunamis

she is trying to tell us

don't you see

we need to stop

stop this madness

of harmful actions

before she gives up on us

today

zooming in you will see the earth

yelling out dead silence

axes chop down the throats of the soil

withering society in a dying world

viral epidemic spread through hushed bees

using our mother

treacherous miles destroyed

singing that somber song

rain cries with us

quadrants exposed in a spotlight

purposeful decay

order this destruction

the people

moving away

lavishing greens that

jumping in time

in the breezy forest

hummingbirds tumbling down

grass still singing a somber song

fallen trees lay hopeless

environment gone then

drought engulfing the scenery

crippling fears for foe as

biology at its finest

animals peer through

universe

balancing the eyes on your face

as you gaze into the breathing balls of energy

feel the explosion

peering into a black hole

a supernova

from seventh grade science class

feel it erupt

birthing stars into the atmosphere

epilogue

the brain can only guide you toward your sensory strip, but you have to walk it alone. my inspiration for this collection comes from late-night thoughts that pop out of the ceiling from staring at it too long. i unraveled these thoughts into this collection of poetry. poetry has taken me on a journey and showed me how to express myself through art and literature. with this collection, i created content directed toward teenagers and young adults. the underrepresentation of published youth poetry astounded me. i hope by creating this piece, other youth poets and writers will publish beautiful works for the world to see. walk into the present, the world is awaiting your gift.

acknowledgement

i would like to thank my mother. she has encouraged me to publish this collection from day one. she is my main supporter. to my dad, the problem solver. thank you for giving me insight on every aspect and helping this book grow. thank you to my friend, the one that believed in me every step of the way. to cat mccarrey, for helping me make sense of my thoughts. to many writers including: rupi kaur, catarine hancock, amanda lovelace and r.h. sin. through your works, i have been inspired to write my own. thank you to everyone in my life for shaping my past and present so that i could experience the marvels that the world has to offer.

about the author

Sejal Akerkar

sejal akerkar is a fifteen-year-old sophomore in high school. born in new york city and after two pit stops in philadelphia and india, sejal finally made her home in bellevue, washington. this is the author's first poetry collection. as a teenager, she strives to write poetry from the youth perspective. she is a proud member of the young writers cohort at hugo house, an organization for serious writers. she has participated in many acts of service around her community and will keep serving. she is a dignified sister, daughter, and friend. through her collection, she explores her path through life and hopes to connect with the sensory strip of others.

Made in the USA
Middletown, DE
08 December 2020